Emotional Bankruptcy

The Economics of Being Too Nice

Lucille C. Gambardella, PhD, APN-BC, CNE, ANEF

PAGE PUBLISHING, INC.
Conneaut Lake, PA

First originally published by Page Publishing 2019

ISBN 978-1-64544-658-3 (pbk)
ISBN 978-1-64544-659-0 (digital)

Printed in the United States of America

This book is dedicated to my husband, Bob, and two daughters, Gina and Andrea. You all have contributed to my healthy emotional status over the years of your love and giving of yourselves to our family. In addition, I dedicate this book to the many women who crossed the threshold of my office practice to rebuild your lives and restore your emotional solvency.

CONTENTS

f.   Investing in yourself daily
g.   Saving for a rainy day

Chapter 6:   Emotional Solvency
a.   Setting the stage
b.   Making the changes
c.   Maintaining the new role

Chapter 7:   The Solvent You

INTRODUCTION

I wish I could take the credit for coining the term "emotional bank-ruptcy," but I cannot. The credit belongs to F. Scott Fitzgerald who, at a low point in his life, wrote a series of articles for *Esquire* magazine in 1936. In these articles—"The Crack Up," "Pasting It Together," and "Handle with Care," and the final article actually entitled "Emotional Bankruptcy" about a woman named Josephine, who spends all her emotional energy and, when the right man comes along, has no energy to feel love for him—the focus point was Fitzgerald's concept of emotional bankruptcy, which he defined as using up one's capacity for emotion and being left with nothing, drawing on resources you do not have. In a nutshell, that is what this book is about.

Over the past forty years that I practiced as a psychotherapist, after treating many clients, like Josephine in Fitzgerald's work, who suffered from what I diagnosed as emotional bankruptcy. They came to my practice, identifying their problem as depression, and most of them were women—women who described their symptoms as inability to sleep, sadness, lack of energy, loss of interest in the things and people around them, and poor self-confidence and belief in their own personal value. These symptoms are indeed indications of depression in many persons.

The typical client I treated for this malady was between twenty-three to forty-seven years of age, with a wide range of educational backgrounds, from high school to postgraduate degrees. A large majority were divorced or single; some were currently married, but described their marriages as "less than good." Medication and psycho-therapy were used as interventions at first. However, a large majority of these women, who would normally respond to pharmacological intervention, with a variety of antidepressants in combination with psychotherapy, did *not* respond with a decrease in symptoms and a return to normal life. When this happened time after time, I decided that there had to be something else happening in the dynamics of this select group. What was different about these women? Why weren't a variety of antidepressants working as with other depressed clients? What was I missing in the dynamics I was seeing? All of these questions stimulated my thinking and desire to gather more information so that I could successfully treat them.

So I decided to more closely examine the trail of cases to determine common elements that could be pointing to an explanation beyond that in the depression dynamic. My research was designed to validate a nonpharmacological means to restore a sense of self in these women by helping them to invest in themselves and their future. I truly believed that their status was not "pathological," but a role they chose to play in their interaction with others. It affected their relationships at work, in their family, and in their romantic encounters.

Therefore, I began to approach current clients with a different treatment plan in mind, one that more fully explored the relationships of the client across the spectrum of family, workplace, and intimate situations and offered them an alternative choice of role to implement. I looked for patterns of relationship behavior that were common in all interactive environments the client experienced. For several years I gathered qualitative data that resulted in my decision to diagnose an amazing number of women (very few men fit the category) with emotional bankruptcy. Interventions I utilized with this select group centered around leaving the emotionally bankrupt role and embracing a new role of holistic sense of self-worth, recognizing the value of reciprocal relationships in all environments, and appreciating the worth of what they have to offer to others without feeling used and disrespected.

I have attempted, in this book, to share with you my findings and the interventions that will help you to change this unhealthy method of interaction with others. Emotional bankruptcy is a learned process, and as such, it can be unlearned. There is a remedial process that can reverse the destructive processes now controlling your life, resulting in your feelings of sadness, poor self-worth, and depleted emotional energy. It is not necessary to spend another day in a relationship mode that does not permit feelings of fulfillment, joy, and personal rewards that enhance your life. Emotional bankruptcy reduces the quality of life and daily performance and diminishes the working and social relationships one has with other people.

If you are reading this book because you believe that you, too, suffer from emotional bankruptcy and that it is time to replenish your emotional bank account and move forward in your life to happier and more satisfying relationships, begin today to make the changes needed to take an alternate path in your life, a path that brings joy, a sense of self that is positive, and a future filled with reciprocal relationships that build energy and self-confidence. If you are not sure, I would hope by the end of this book, you will be able to determine a personal assessment that puts you on the road toward solvency and meaningful, rewarding relationships across the spectrum of your life.

The goals of this book are simple:

1. To help the reader recognize if the characteristics of emotional bankruptcy are inherent in them
2. To understand how emotional bankruptcy is interfering with their personal growth and development and overall happiness
3. To determine those effective intervention strategies that work for them to overcome the bankruptcy and restore emotional solvency

The framework of this book parallels the financial phenomenon of bankruptcy. The terminology of the financial process is highly relevant to the phenomenon of emotional bankruptcy, and its familiar terms will hopefully make it easier to understand what is happening in your life. The book will explore emotional bankruptcy from a perspective of declaring bankruptcy (chapter 11), examining the emotional spending processes, setting up a plan to get out of debt, including debt consolidation, and the important steps of paying yourself first, collecting interest, overdraft protection, building an emotional 401K, investing in yourself, and "saving" for a rainy day.

Let's begin the journey!

CHAPTER 1

The Essential Elements of the Emotional Bankruptcy Phenomenon

The phenomenon of emotional bankruptcy is a fascinating set of dynamics that influence behaviors of many women who have difficulty establishing and maintaining healthy relationships in many avenues of their lives. It is helpful to try to understand the underlying dynamics of these behaviors prior to investigating emotional bankruptcy itself in subsequent chapters. During the research process with the clients in my practice, three major dynamic concepts were identified that proved to be the foundations for the dysfunctional relationship pattern: inability to establish boundaries, ineffective methods of meeting emotional needs, and issues of control. I will explain each of these and the role they play in the economics of being too nice.

Boundaries are important is any relationship, whether at home, at work or with a significant other. Boundaries provide the limits within which the relationship functions and boundaries allow each person in the relationship to recognize where they end and the other person begins. Further, boundaries provide the parameters for healthy interaction. Recognizing the extent of boundaries allows a person to know when to "stay in their lane", to identify when they are overstepping and becoming intrusive in their relationships. It is easy to violate boundaries when one feels insecure or does not recognize the value of self. Many times, overstepping boundaries is misconstrued as being helpful or giving advice (albeit unsolicited!) Unclear boundaries, particularly in family relationships, can mean duplication or blurring of roles which can be confusing in family dynamics. For example, when a child in a family becomes the dominant individual in determining decisions in the family rather than the parent, chaos ensues. The parent might feel threatened by the child or perhaps unable to provide the determined discipline needed to keep order. As you read through the book, you will see that this is an issue in intimate or work relationships as well. Overstepping boundaries on a regular basis leads to frustration, feelings of helplessness and anger because the recipient of the overstepping is not getting what they need out of the relationship. It is easy to see then that when boundaries are not respected, emotions can be depleted with little source of replenishment from the relationship partner as the give and take of normal boundaries does not exist.

Ineffective methods of meeting emotional needs are the second important element to understand in the dynamics of relationships. In healthy relationships, the individual players are able to let the relationship partner know when they need something. Ideally they voice that need out loud: "I need you to stop doing that because it makes me angry when you do" or "I am exhausted from this stress and I need to be alone to relax for an hour". These expressions are "I" based, say what the need is and denotes how the need will be met. Vocalizing needs are a meaningful method for self-care and do not place blame on the other partner in the relationship. Instead, vocalizing in the above manner puts responsibility within the person who has the need to identify it and satisfy it in some way acceptable to them. An unhealthy method of meeting emotional needs involves blame of the relationship partner or not verbalizing the need yet expecting the relationship partner "to know" the need is present and therefore satisfy it without asking. Isn't that a magical event that should happen???!!! Yet, how often do we do that, we assume the other person should know what we need if they care about us. In my practice, I often heard clients say, especially in couple's therapy, "why should I have to ask him to give me some quiet time, if he cares about me, he should know I need that after a long day at work". No, he's not required to know, if you need that you need to ask for it. Other ineffective ways of meeting emotional needs is to manipulate others using guilt to attain what is needed. For example, "you never help me around this house, if I drop over from a heart attack doing this heavy work you'll be sorry"...or perhaps stating in a martyr, whining tone..."never mind, I'll do it myself". Utilizing guilt is a poor method of having needs met, especially in family or marital relationships. It builds anger, low self-esteem and an overwhelming fear of being abandoned in the relationship. The person experiencing emotional bankruptcy is a victim of many of these feelings on an every-day basis. The stress of those feelings and sense of inadequacy is common ground for the feelings of depression and sadness felt in the emotional bankruptcy phenomenon.

Finally, the issue of control in the dynamics of relationships. Later in the book we look at locus of control and why it is important in understanding emotional bankruptcy and the steps needed to regain solvency. However, control, in general, is always a key element in how relationships evolve. To some, control means power and strength. To others, control is a method of operation to guaranteeing of that control (the person being controlled) feels inadequate and the victim of the person who is in control. In addition, HOW the control is implemented can make a major difference in how it is tolerated. Physical control, through abuse or violence, for example, is unacceptable and much more difficult to escape from by the person being abused. The dynamics of abuse are too complex to address here, but it is important to know that control is an issue in emotional bankruptcy that should be addressed as soon as it is recognized. Control, however, does not have to be physical to be a problem in a relationship. Often it rears its ugly head in much more subtle ways that make it difficult to recognize. In many ways playing the victim, common in emotional bankruptcy, is a method of control the woman uses to keep a relationship alive. This method of control however, saps the energy and life from one's emotional bank account and soon depletes all reserves with no hope for emotional replenishment.

Together, the above three elements are all players in the cycle of emotional bankruptcy. Each contributes, in its own way, to the dysfunctional relationships in the life of the emotionally bankrupt person. This is the journey you are about to explore.

CHAPTER 2

The Economics of Being Too Nice

Emotional bankruptcy takes a devastating toll on the lives of millions of women across the world. It inhibits the natural growth and flow of relationships in the workplace, in families, and in intimate dyads. But it does not have to exist; it can be eradicated if women are amenable to learning the dynamics behind their behavior and the interventions that can help them to enjoy fulfillment and happiness in how they relate to others.

Emotional bankruptcy is what I define as a depletion of emotional energy as a result of maintaining nonreciprocal interpersonal relationships. Further, relationships fail to replenish emotional resources that satisfy personal needs. As women, we are socialized for caring, giving, and nonaggression. Emotional bankruptcy is a cycle of learned behaviors and, to some extent, is an extension of the "nurturing" values instilled in women. We are supposed to be caring, supposed to be understanding and forgiving, right? As a result, the woman develops symptoms of emotional bankruptcy across three categories: feelings, behaviors, and unhealthy relationships.

Feeling symptoms include frustration, helplessness, anger, and low self-esteem. The feeling of frustration results from the inability of the woman to establish a lasting, meaningful relationship. The emotionally bankrupt person eventually finds their relationships end, and they end badly. The partner usually terminates the relationship with a sense of disgust—a disgust that emanates from the emotionally bankrupt partner being a pushover, a whiner, and someone unable to be proud of or have respect for within the relationship.

Consider this example: Liz often fought with her boyfriend of five years, and every argument ended up in the same direction with him saying to her, "You are such a waste. I don't even know why I stay with you. You have nothing to offer to anybody, especially me." This always worked to bring Liz to tears and to feel unworthy of being with this man and eventually apologizing to him for the source of argument. At the same time, her boyfriend continued to feel superior to her and reinforced the way he treated her in the relationships. A win-win for him, and a lose-lose for Liz. Women are inherently nurturing and socialized for caring, giving, and nonaggression. The women's movement improved this somewhat, but many women still fall into this socialization process of being a giver rather than a taker. One important move I taught my clients is that you have to build a solid playbook of ways to interact so that you can ensure revenue integrity in your emotional life. This prevents situations of an overdraft in your assets and builds resilience.

This process, repeated over and over in a relationship, leads to the three other feelings of helplessness, anger, and low self-esteem. The woman cannot help but feel helpless since partners leave her. She becomes angry over not seemingly having any control over the situation, and the repeated losses lead to low self-esteem and feelings of worthlessness. As the situation replays itself, the cycle appears to be endless, with no way to break its momentum. A self-inflicted level of victimization develops that becomes debilitating and immobilizing. Some typical comments I heard from my patients included "Jack is not always kind to me, but he works so hard and is just tired" or "My boss is traveling a lot, so he has delegated a lot of his extra work to me, and I feel obligated to pick it up even though it gives me a twelve-hour workday" and "When you are a mother, you are just not in control of your life…your husband or your kids determine what you need." Such sad statements of thinking that indicate the feelings of being a victim.

A victim is a person who suffers from a destructive or injurious action, either self-inflicted or inflicted, by someone else. Synonyms include nouns such as martyr, pawn, pushover, a fool; none of which are in any way flattering. The word victim comes from the Latin word *victima*, which translates to "sacrificial animal." The women seen in my practice fit this scenario and exhibited behaviors characteristic of victimization. The goal, as you will see later in the book, is to reverse the role of victimization to the role of empowerment. The table below further clarifies the behavior changes desired in the intervention process.

Victimized	Empowered
Passive	Courageous
Pushover	Strong conviction
Pawn	Self-confident

Behavior symptoms are the most complex component of the emotional-bankruptcy cycle. Most women are not cognizant of the role they play in enacting these behaviors, and they are even less aware that they can control and change these behaviors if they desire to do so. But I will discuss these in chapter 3.

The first of these nonproductive behaviors is the violation of boundaries. In healthy relationships, both partners respect the boundaries of the other. This healthy respect indicates caring and valuing of each other. It says, "I will not overstep my bounds in what I expect or how I treat you. I will see us not only as a couple, but as individuals with rights, needs, and reasonable expectations." The emotionally bankrupt woman is unable (or unwilling) to acknowledge the lack of respect for boundaries by her partner and responds to the ongoing demands of the partner who consistently has his needs met but ignores the needs of the woman. The woman mistakenly believes that things will get better if "he just gets that new big client" or "his father finally gives him some recognition" or a million other excuses. The bottom line is that, basing your emotional status on these assumptions will continue to spiral you into further emotional debt. A balanced emotional budget cannot be based on assumptions but must be based on realistic emotional needs. For example, in a realistic financial budget, expenses are determined on the basis of a salary earned and the intent to save at least a little with each paycheck if you can. This allows the individual to build good credit and to plan for a rainy day. Likewise, an emotional budget must have the same realistic behaviors that satisfy personal emotional needs through positive feedback, such as compliments, good works, self-care, and reciprocal relationships that add deposits to your emotional bank account, as well as build self-esteem for a "rainy day." Withdrawals quickly deplete assets if you do not make regular deposits, and such is the case in the emotionally bankrupt person.

This leads to the second of the behavior symptoms, which is the inability to express personal needs. The emotionally bankrupt woman, because of low self-esteem, cannot express what it is she needs to maintain her emotional bank account. Her sense of unworthiness encourages her to put her partner's needs first and foremost to the detriment of her need to be fulfilled. This behavior feeds the feelings of anger and helplessness described above. It also is a signal that it is time to be on an emotional budget, which includes increasing emotional income through more positive relationships at all levels. Emotionally bankrupt women need to find new sources of emotional income and refuel. Maintaining positive boundaries and expressing personal needs will facilitate that emotional income. Other emotional income comes from paying yourself first emotionally through both physical and mental self-care. Meditation, yoga, relaxation techniques, exercise, new experiences, such as travel, taking a class, and choosing a new hobby are only a few of the ways you can improve your emotional income and keep your account solvent. Think of these as emotional fitness exercises and a component of critical life skills. All these things improve the energies expended in our everyday lives at home, at work, or in social settings and build constructive thinking. If you cannot remember the last time you did something just for yourself, it is time to address that missing element in your life. I encouraged "queen for a day" events to my clients and supported the positive outcomes those events brought about. Something as simple as a manicure/pedicure just because, not for a special occasion is an example of taking care of the inner self and not leaving it up to someone else to do so. You are responsible for your own happiness and rewards. Remember that internal locus of control!

Violation of boundaries and the inability to express personal needs and the resultant anger and helplessness create the perfect storm for nonproductive communication, the third behavioral symptom. Each of us knows how difficult it is to communicate when one is angry or feels helpless. Instead of rational interaction, it is easy to whine, to complain, to attack the other person with irrational comments and angry accusations. This nonproductive form of communicating is a critical result of the emotionally bankrupt relationship and serves to force the individuals in the relationship even further apart.

The final behavioral symptom is the woman's unconscious need for control. In her effort to be in control, the dynamics to achieve that status become reversed and allow the partner to control her with demands and high expectations she can't possibly achieve within the relationship. This behavior, which can occur in an intimate relationship, in the workplace, or in a family, is highly characteristic of the emotionally bankrupt woman. However, control is never achieved, and the woman feels at the mercy of the other person in the relationship.

Given the first two sets of symptoms, feelings, and behaviors, it will be simple to understand the overall characteristics of the third set of symptoms, which are the relationships themselves. The emotionally bankrupt relationship demonstrates no reciprocity, energy depletion, immaturity, and unsatisfactory outcomes.

Lack of reciprocity is a logical characteristic in that the relationship with an emotionally bankrupt woman is totally one-sided. She is the giver, and the other relationship participant is the taker. In her need to feel good and worthy and to receive love, she is willing to give until she can give no more. This was evident in each of the women I treated over the years…but never could they understand how the relationship ended. "How could they leave me?" "How could they fire me?" or "Why does my family leave me out of the loop when I do everything for everybody?" The possibility of her setting the stage for this to happen was never a consideration! Yet in chapter 3 when we examine the journey into bankruptcy, these dynamics will become evident.

It is only natural to see how this lack of reciprocity leads to the emotionally bankrupt woman feeling energy depleted. Her emotional bank account never takes in "deposits." Think of how your bill paying process would be a disaster if you never made deposits into your checking account. You would be bouncing checks all over the place. In a similar manner, the emotionally bankrupt woman draws on insufficient energy to maintain relationships that do not provide income or dividends. She is never able to replenish her resources because she is too busy giving and never seizes the opportunity to be on the taking side. Energy depletion leads to feelings of fatigue, restlessness, and lack of interest in everyday living activities. My women clients often would describe themselves as "out if it" or "just not able to do even simple things," which made them feel useless and even unworthy of being alive.

The final two relationship characteristics, immaturity and unsatisfactory outcomes, piggyback on one another. When an emotionally bankrupt woman is in a relationship in any setting, her interactions with others tend to be childlike and immature as she exerts efforts to be taken care of by others. However, this approach backfires and puts her into the position of always caring for others. It is interesting to note that as I researched this behavior over the years, it became evident that the emotionally bankrupt woman chose relationships with those who she could sense would be demanding, have high unrealistic expectations, and often would be demeaning. It is almost a self-fulfilling prophecy that does not allow for a satisfactory outcome and good feelings resulting from the relationship. Unfortunately, the repetitious pattern of choices requires an intervention to break the cycle and to learn new behaviors and new roles to be enacted to relationships at all levels.

CHAPTER 3

The Journey into Bankruptcy

My work as a therapist was to help the emotionally bankrupt woman out of emotional debt, similar to how a credit counselor would help someone headed into financial bankruptcy. I often felt like an emotional debt coach! As I worked with each woman, I recognized the cycle of emotional bankruptcy. My goal was to help them recognize this cycle and to break it: Below is how the cycle of emotional bankruptcy works:

emotional bankruptcy

poor self esteem and fear of abandonment

self inflicted victimization with ineffective relationships

lack of reciprocity and mutuality

depleted assets due to no emotional deposits

This a cycle of learned behaviors that can become debilitating and immobilizing for those caught in its clutches.

The dynamics that make this cycle possible is a woman who is unable to recognize the value of mutuality or reciprocity in any relationship. Out of her fear of the other person leaving her and the resulting abandonment, she feels the need to consistently give to others to keep them in her world. However, this behavior dynamic results in the emotionally bankrupt woman being stuck in the role of being a victim. Any victim knows the feelings that go along with this role, and they are draining, destructive, and nonproductive.

Does anyone know anyone who enjoys being in the company of a victim? I must say that I do not. They are a drain on your being. They are tiring, and you feel frustrated because despite their complaints, they do not make any effort to change that victim status. I believe we all have been in toxic relationships, be it friendships, work relationships, or family dyads, where one person always plays the victim. It is not pleasant, and we are more likely to avoid the "victim" than embrace them in an ongoing relationship. This is what the emotionally bankrupt woman experiences. Instead of her constant giving bringing positive results, it creates negative feelings and expressions of her lack of sense of self. In order to exit this role and move to a new, healthier role of positive and rewarding relationships and a return to emotional solvency, something has to change. It is pure economics: like a bank account, you cannot just take withdrawals, you must make regular deposits in your emotional bank account. Reversing the process to create positive economics and solvency involves a teaching process. It is evident to me as a therapist, that some women learn this role early in childhood in relationships with parents and siblings. Sometimes it is a result of a need to please others. Later in life, they transfer those behaviors to all of their other relationships because it is comfortable, it is what they know and are familiar with despite the fact that the behaviors bring them no joy. Teaching ways to keep the emotional bank rich in assets is a process that involves changes in thinking, attitudes and behaviors.

The journey into bankruptcy does not occur overnight. It is often a good part of a lifetime that passes before the bankruptcy evolves. As a therapist, before treating an emotionally bankrupt woman, it was necessary to explore the possible theoretical dynamics that contribute to its evolution as well as to its treatment. I want to briefly explain these here so as you read this book, you too will see what contributes to this phenomenon. I did not see these clients as having a DSM pathology, rather as someone who needed to adopt a new role within relationships that would enhance their emotional well-being. I would encourage further reading on the following constructs to enhance the brief explanations found here.

A discussion of the concept of locus of control initiates this review. There are two options for locus of control: internal and external. Internal locus of control is a belief by an individual that he/she determines what occurs in life. Choices are made, goals are set, outcomes are facilitated. In other words, responsibility and accountability for what happens in life are accepted. Those with internal locus of control make conscious choices often based on consideration of previous experiences, knowledge, and input of others. When failure results, they examine the possible reasons why, learn from the events and move on. On the other hand, an individual who believes in an external locus of control believes that outside events in our environment determine what happens in life. For those with an external locus of control, if something goes wrong, it is someone else or something else that made it go wrong. There is little or no personal accountability or responsibility for what occurs in life. Therefore, those with external locus of control often repeat poor choices and expect different results. They do not examine poor outcomes for plausible causes but instead believe "other" factors are the reason for failure. Thus, the person with an external locus of control finds it very easy to be a "victim," whether a victim of other people or a victim of circumstance. Thus, the victim role is born and enacted as a personality trend—a trend that blends into the emotionally bankrupt woman. The following is a perfect example of this external locus of control mentality: Jill was a twenty-seven-year-old midlevel executive in a large company. She was in a relationship with a thirty-year-old salesman, Kevin, who was married with two young children but described his marriage as "just about over." At our session in October, Jill told me that they had agreed that after the Christmas holiday was over, he would ask his wife for a divorce so that they could be married. Jill was ecstatic and began planning their wedding in her mind for the following fall. Things appeared to be going well until mid-January when she arrived for her appointment, looking frazzled and despondent. As we began the session, she began to cry softly and told me that Kevin said they would have to postpone their plans and that he had not asked for a divorce as previously planned. His son was having problems at school, and Kevin just didn't think it was the right time. When I asked Jill how she felt about this, she stated, "It is disappointing, but I feel so sorry for his little boy, and he needs his dad... It's not Kevin's fault that this happened right now." Unfortunately, this happened three times in the life of the relationship before Kevin broke off the relationship telling her he could not tolerate her nagging about wanting to get married!

This leads to the second process used in understanding and assisting the emotionally bankrupt woman. The sociological theory of Ebaugh called the Process of Role Exit sparked my interest as I researched this behavioral phenomenon. Behavior is a learned process. Psychology tells us that over and over in numerous articles, books, and television shows. The role we choose to play in life is also learned and can be unlearned. Role-exit theory expands upon this process and clarifies that the emotionally bankrupt woman who learned to play this role can also learn to play a new role that enhances the ability to create healthy relationships and to experience the joy and reward of positive relationships.

How one relearns this role utilizes the concepts of cognitive restructuring and cognitive behavioral therapy. Cognitive restructuring is the management of negative thinking. It is a process where what we tell ourselves and how we interpret our environment can be changed. If we change our assumptions and interpretations, we can change our thinking. Psychology tells us that our moods are directly driven by how we think, so if we retrain our minds to think positively, we can change both our role and our behavior as we interact with others. This is of particular interest when we think about how women operate to get their needs met. In Chapter 1, we looked at the ways a person can choose to achieve having their needs met. Vocalizing the need and asking for what is needed or using guilt and manipulation were comparisons of healthy and unhealthy methods, respectively. If the emotionally bankrupt woman is accustomed to employing unhealthy ways to having needs met, new ways can be learned as part of assuming a new role on the way to emotional solvency. In therapy with clients, I often had them practice during our session the new behaviors and how change could improve their relationships and bring them out of bankruptcy. This is a helpful method for building emotional reserves and making deposits into one's emotional bank account.

Utilizing these three theories of dynamics, the goals of non-pharmacologic interventions for the emotionally bankrupt woman became simple:

- Restore solvency.
- Build an emotional 401K.
- Maintain a balanced emotional budget.

However, before this process can begin, a declaration of bankruptcy must be made. This first step in resolving any problem that interferes with our living a life of fulfillment is the most difficult. Just as the alcoholic must declare himself as an alcoholic, the emotionally bankrupt woman must admit that she is in a state of uncontrollable emotional debt. Chapter 4 will take you through that process.

CHAPTER 4

Declaring Bankruptcy

Admitting that you are in uncontrollable emotional debt is the difficult first step in facilitating the change required to achieve emotional solvency. When working with my clients, I would often refer to this process as filing chapter 11, which, in the financial world, is a reorganization process to assess the exact status of your situation and possibly negotiating a restructuring plan. From an emotional standpoint, it is the process of evaluating the relationships in your life to determine which are toxic and draining your emotional account and which are healthy and contributing to your emotional account. This can be a difficult process as it requires a level of objectivity often elusive for the emotionally bankrupt person.

However, it is essential if you want to have a fresh start toward solvency. Eliminating those relationships that are dysfunctional is like selling off the assets when our liabilities exceed our assets. It is an attempt to restore our emotional funds and to build some equity. Often the decision to seek therapy is the initial step in admitting emotional bankruptcy.

As I reviewed the cases I counseled through the years, it was not uncommon for these clients to identify themselves as "hopeless," "not knowing where to turn next," or "sick of being taken in by the users of the world." One client, who had been in her fifth relationship with a man who she described as "egotistical and conniving," questioned me, saying, "Why do I always end up with this kind of man... What is wrong with me?" As a therapist, it was not unusual for me to respond to questions like that by encouraging the client to do some reflection so that she could begin to answer that question for herself.

As you are reading this book, this may need to be your first step, *reflection*. The initial assessment questionnaire I devised for the emotional bankruptcy client follows below. I would encourage you to take some time to go through the questionnaire and carefully answer the questions honestly after reflecting on your current status.

Initial Assessment Questionnaire for Emotional Bankruptcy

Name: _____

Date of Birth: _____

Marital Status: S_____M_____D_____Cohabit_____

Education: High School____ Some College____
College Degree____ Grad Degree ____

Race: White____ Non-Hispanic____
Hispanic____ African American____ Other ____

Why have you come for treatment today?

Describe your symptoms.

Describe what you have tried to help yourself.

Are you currently taking any medications?

Have you been in therapy before? If so, describe the results.

Tell me about your usual decision-making/problem-solving methods.

Describe your predominant mood.

Tell me about your usual methods for getting your needs met in any relationship.

What are your greatest strengths?

What are your greatest weaknesses?

What do you wish to accomplish in this treatment process?

Tell me anything else you feel is important for me to know about you before you begin this treatment process.

Using the results of your personal assessment can help you to position yourself for change. If you were honest in assessing your assets and liabilities, readiness to move from the victim role within your emotional bankruptcy will set the stage to enable you to take time out to consider the behaviors that will move your old role as a victim to your new role of strength, power, and control over your life. Review the victimization table in the previous chapter 2. It was noted earlier that your journey into bankruptcy did not occur overnight, so you must have patience while building a new path to solvency. This new path involves setting realistic goals for future relationships, having a positive sense of self-esteem, and building your plan to get out of emotional debt. Think of it as being on a "mental budget." A financial budget means you tighten your belt for a while, and you avoid unnecessary spending. The same applies here. Consider every bit of emotional spending before it occurs, be conservative in how you facilitate your relationships, and whether there is a positive reciprocity in those relationships.

Part of getting out of emotional debt is exploring how you are spending your emotional energy. This requires that you maintain a balance sheet to assist you in learning how to control the give and take in your relationships. At this point, your spending is likely out of balance, with heavy emphasis on the giving process with little replenishment of resources from the taking side. Consider this balance sheet similar to how you balance your checkbook with the knowledge that you cannot spend what you do not have! Avoid overdrafts on your emotional energy with the same tenacity as you balance your financial assets. Below is a sample balance sheet tool that can assist you to keep track of your emotional spending. Use it as you begin your reorganization to functional relationships in your life.

Emotional Bankruptcy Balance Sheet and Journal

Date/Time	Mood/Feeling	Event	Cause	Withdrawal or Deposit	Net gain or Loss

Another aspect of declaring bankruptcy is establishing a commitment to a time frame. As I observed with so many of my clients, the initial feeling was expressed similar to that of when we want to go on a diet, with comments such as "I'll start next week" or "I want to give him/her/my sister/my coworker another chance." Yes, the emotionally bankrupt person is always ready to "give another chance" despite the fact that it is at her own expense! Readiness is key to success, and commitment to learning new behaviors is what unlocks the cycle of bankruptcy. In therapy, I took clients through this process of determining readiness. Readiness is key to understanding *how* to facilitate change in thinking and behaviors. If the person is not ready, there is more likely there will be resistance to the change. There are five stages of readiness: (1) not yet considering change due to denial or possible "giving up"; (2) ambivalent about change and sees too many barriers to change; (3) willing to try small suggestions for change; (4) taking definitive steps to alter behavior; and (5) continuing the new behavior and abandoning the old (DiClemente and Prochaska 1998). If there is any relapse in the process, likelihood is a return to the old behavior. A quick way to visually determine your level of readiness can be determined by picturing a simple ruler used in math. At one end is not prepared to change, and at the other, already changing. You can mark where on the ruler you currently are, and then adjust as your behaviors move toward readiness.

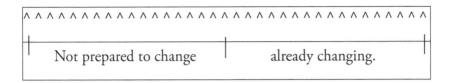

Not prepared to change | already changing.

Just as there are steps in the process of readiness, change also has stages that occur. Many clients proceeded through these stages several times before actually achieving change, but that is okay. Old behaviors are tough to give up, even if they are uncomfortable, they are familiar. The stages of change are the following:

First, precontemplation. In this stage, as a therapist, I did a lot of educating the patient relative to the ways in which the behaviors were effecting lifestyle, achievement of happiness, etc. The education was geared toward improving awareness and building confidence in the ability to create change.

Second, contemplation. At this stage, the client and I spent time identifying misconceptions in beliefs about self and the other partner in the relationships; clarifying what was reality and what was fantasy based on an objective review of events in the relationship.

Third, preparation. This stage involved developing goals and actually building a time line for change. It involved making a realistic plan with the client in small steps that each led toward the decision to create the change.

Fourth, action. This stage required extensive support from me for any behavioral changes then moved away from the emotionally bankrupt status toward self-solvency. Strong reinforcement for efforts to alter behavior and response to negative behaviors is important and encouraging self-affirmations on a daily basis all help to maintain this stage of change.

Fifth, maintenance. Perhaps the most difficult of the stages as the client often felt frustrated if "life" didn't get better immediately despite the changes being made.

Looking at the stages of readiness and stages of change together can help you understand how the mind operates when exiting a familiar role to adopt a new role in life. It does take time and patience, but the rewards of a positive self-image, confidence, and a return to emotional solvency are improved quality of life and opportunities for relationships that bring joy and love into life. So take the step to being ready now, and let's get to work.

CHAPTER 5

Getting out of Emotional Debt and Building Solvency

I will assume you are ready to get out of emotional debt. This means you have filed an emotional chapter 11 and have called a time-out to focus on changing your behaviors. This is the time to prepare a reorganization plan that will allow that change to happen. The reorganization plan is realistic, futuristic, and user-friendly for you and your goals. It commits to a time frame and honestly assesses your assets and liabilities.

The major rules of your reorganization plan are perhaps a new challenge to you. They consist of transitioning to a new spending and debt-consolidation process of paying yourself first, making regular deposits into your emotional account, and building equity for an emotionally secure life. This is the time I often recommended that my clients keep a daily journal so that they could keep track of the changes being made and investments and interests earned in their emotional bankruptcy journey. If you need to do so, review the journal outline in the previous chapter.

In the past, you have likely never thought about how you spend your emotional dollars; you looked at your resources as never-ending so that there was no need to be frugal or save for a rainy day! Now that will change as you raise your awareness to the negative behaviors controlling your interactions. You will *think* about how you spend those emotional dollars prior to investing in others. Thus, you will *always* pay yourself first; translated, that means your emotional needs come first so that you have the energy and resources to care for self and care for others without overdrafts on your account. Think of it like being on an airplane and being told to put on your oxygen mask first, then put the mask on your child. Same principle is in play as you cannot save others if you don't safe yourself first; not selfish, just practical and realistic.

Once you become comfortable with this principle of paying yourself first, it will become second nature and part of assuming a new role in relationships. This payment of self first also allows an opportunity for debt consolidation. You will take a closer look at all your relationships and consider those that are draining your account and begin to clear the slate of relationships that don't provide reciprocity and opportunities to grow and develop. Liquidating these relationships is not selfish. They are a strong affirmation of your self-confidence and renewed self-esteem. As the debts are consolidated and eliminated, new and regular deposits will be made into your emotional account, and you will feel refreshed, renewed, and emotionally strong. The account's equity, solvency, and an emotionally secure life will slowly evolve, and you will discover that your relationships are satisfying and meaningful.

Paying yourself first produces an emotional 401k. An emotional 401k ensures your emotional integrity like a retirement 401k provides savings for retirement. At a time in your life when income is diminished, the 401k ensures an income from interest and principal that has grown over the years and allows you to continue to live comfortably without a dependency on others. Your emotional 401k is an investment in yourself so that when stressful times emerge, or relationships are challenging, you have the emotional reserves to move forward and maintain an emotionally secure life.

The emotional 401k is about improving self-esteem. It uses that personal assessment and reorganization plan you created during the time you filed for chapter 11. Improving self-esteem includes the utilization of self-affirmations, practicing positive and assertive communication exercises, and learning to say no. Consider these to be emotional fitness exercises. Strengthening the brain and its function—fostering constructive thinking with empathetic honesty and learning critical life skills.

When working with my clients in psychotherapy, we would practice self-affirmations in my office until the client was comfortable doing them at home. Some of the key phrases I would teach them to use included "I am a good person," "I deserve to be treated with respect and love," "I can achieve my goal (then say the goal)," and "I am strong and intelligent." There are many others that can be used in this exercise, and it is helpful to gear the affirmations to those qualities that you need to improve. Say the affirmations into a mirror, and watch your body language and facial expressions; the nonverbals are just as important as the verbal content.

Other components of self-affirmations include teaching assertive behaviors within communication patterns. Do you find yourself apologizing a lot when you speak? Is the apology necessary, or just an indication of poor self-worth? Do you use self-deprecation and diminish your worth by describing personal weaknesses, even ones that don't exist? Do you often speak in such a soft-voice volume that others can barely here you, as if what you are saying is not worth hearing anyway? All these behaviors are common in the woman who is experiencing emotional bankruptcy. So in addition to saying those self-affirmations, stop apologizing needlessly! Increase that voice volume so that you are confident in what you have to say, and stop the self-deprecation. Use "I" statements to describe how you feel. Be proud of your abilities and assets, and when you get a compliment, just say thank you and move forward because you deserve it!

Laughter is also affirming. Healthy four-year-olds laugh about every three to five minutes, adults maybe three to four times a day! That is sad because it indicates that we are too tense and concerned with stress we cannot relax enough to see the lighter side of life. Picture yourself free, use imagery to picture what can be, and then strive to meet that image, that goal.

Practicing assertive communication was also a component of many therapy sessions, and the client and I would role play situations that were a challenge to provide opportunities to try out new communication skills that would indicate personal strength, self-care, and recognition of self-worth. Clients with emotional bankruptcy have particular difficulty saying no to others and overextending themselves to please others, yet put themselves at risk for emotional exhaustion. Some of the role-playing scenarios included others asking for favors like babysitting, driving someone somewhere, or planning and implementing an event that they did not enjoy.

These role-play scenarios led to discussion of the client's feelings of disappointing others, feeling guilty or fear of being abandoned or "unloved" if they said no. The ability to recognize such situations and having the strength to be honest in response to the request is a key factor in overcoming emotional bankruptcy. The ability to say no and realize that it allows you to maintain self-respect and pride in your self-worth is monumental to recovery and change. It is also helpful to understand that if the other person in the relationship ends the relationship because you say no or stand up for yourself, then how good was that relationship in the first place? A relationship that does not allow for honesty and reciprocity in the give-and-take process is a toxic relationship and creates emotional bankruptcy over time, so watch for the red flags and steer clear!

Reciprocity in any relationship is like collecting interest in your financial bank account. As you monitor your bank account, you must also monitor your emotional accounts by assessing the reciprocity and mutuality of your relationships. Keep a journal and look at the debits and credits in your relationships to assess if there is a sharing of needs and concerns. Do you see a lot of one-sided relationships—for example, persons that contact you *only* if they need something? Do you have relationships that leave you feeling void and confused in regard to where you fit in that person's life? Those are the relationships that drain your assets and prevent a balanced emotional budget. Consider those relationships carefully and honestly to determine if they are worth maintaining, and if not, don't be afraid to liquidate and close that account.

There are times when we may choose to keep a relationship despite its lack of reciprocity. Perhaps that relationship is manageable because we are aware of its shortcomings, and you can handle it without guilt or loss of self-respect and self-esteem. It is when most of the relationships have this quality and destroy self-esteem and self-confidence that I recommend that the relationship ends. Many relationships of this type lead to overdrafts, as debits are more plentiful than assets and deposits being made. The rule is zero-based emotional budgeting; this means that all expenses must be justified and approved for each new spending entity. Thus, you must know you can afford this relationship before you move forward. As a result, it is up to you to have an ongoing understanding and knowledge of what your relationships require and provide so that you can determine the income and output of emotional energy and examine if the relationship provides any dividends or interest to add to assets. This ongoing process provides needed change and avoids future episodes of emotional bankruptcy while improving your emotional credit rating.

Maintaining a balanced emotional budget entails other behaviors that improve overall emotional health. It is important to exercise regularly, to eat and sleep in adequate amounts, and to take time just for you. These behaviors contribute to overall wellness and physical health that goes hand in hand with emotional health. Regular exercise, for example, stimulates the brain chemicals that improve mood and feelings of positivity, while good nutrition contributes to cell growth, quality immunity, and system function. As you make emotional deposits into your overall health, the physical deposits are just as essential to breaking the emotional bankruptcy cycle and restoring emotional solvency.

A final suggestion is about connecting to others as a means for building a balanced emotional budget. Today, as a society, we are attached to our electronic gadgets as lifelines for communicating with others. As a therapist, I would be remiss to not comment on the excessive use of cell phones, text messaging, Instagram, Facebook and other systems as THE method for relating to others. All of these tools serve their purpose in today's world, however, when they become a substitute for true, face-to-face interaction our emotional bank suffers. I worry about those who cannot, or will not, take the time to seek out others in person for communication and feedback. Relationships are not electronic, we are not electronic, we are human beings that need eye contact, touch, recognition, smiles, and the warmth that face-to face communication provides. Do not compromise your emotional solvency by diminishing the opportunities for personal interaction with family, in the workplace, or in other meaningful relationships. There is no substitute known to mankind for true healing and a strong sense of emotional well- being. Make those deposits into your emotional bank account count and build that 401K with human experience. The dividends will multiply exponentially.

CHAPTER 6

Emotional Solvency

Investing in yourself daily will be the challenge as you move forward to maintain emotional solvency. This challenge can be overcome with a few simple changes in how you think about yourself and how you live your life. Change is always a challenge, but life is made up of changes. Things never stay the same whether we acknowledge that fact or not. If it is recognized that change is inevitable, it is much easier to anticipate and to face with grace and a certain degree of comfort.

Maintaining emotional solvency is like maintaining a healthy weight—it takes monitoring and some work, but the outcome is worth it because it ensures overall health and wellness. The same will be true for the maintenance of emotional solvency, as the outcome will be overall strong emotional health.

A helpful process that will facilitate ongoing solvency and emotional growth is cognitive restructuring I talked about earlier on in this book. Cognitive restructuring means that you will begin thinking in a different fashion. Research tells us that our moods and self-concept are driven by what we tell ourselves. Cognitive restructuring can help us to change the way we think about situations and also helps us evaluate how valid our thoughts and interpretations of those thoughts are. It is the management of negative thinking. For example, thinking negatively will be replaced by thinking positively. Instead of thinking "I can't do this," you will say "I can do this if I plan carefully and do a, b, or c." When, in any relationship, someone asks you to do something that you do not want to do, instead of gritting your teeth and saying, "Sure, no problem," you will say, "I cannot help you with that this time." No apologies, no excuses, real or otherwise, because remember, you do not need to apologize; you are making a deposit in your emotional bank, not a withdrawal. You will make regular deposits and only withdraw when it is beneficial to you. This objective resource allocation will help you to maintain a fluid account with sufficient assets to manage relationships in a healthy way. It is useful to maintain a cognitive restructuring journal, especially in the beginning of your process for change. The journal should follow these guidelines:

- Write in the journal daily.
- Describe events that trigger negative thoughts.
- Describe how you validated the negative thought.
- List the steps you took to transition to a positive thought.
- Think about the outcome of your effort.
- Describe how the process made you feel.
- Evaluate your progress today.

Your skill-building tool kit for facilitating ongoing solvency and emotional growth also includes a raised awareness to readily accepting the status and role of playing the victim in relationships. The role of victim is a major depleting process that contributes to emotional bankruptcy. A victim role is a passive role, a role that indicates vulnerability and lack of power, and a role that says, "I am in your power, and you can do whatever you want to hurt me, and I am powerless to stop it." That is the old you and the you that will no longer be in vogue. The new, emotionally solvent you will not play the victim role ever again. The new you will be in control of your emotions, empowered to see relationships objectively, and will exit the victim role, and instead assume the role of a strong, productive, happy, and emotionally healthy person who can establish and maintain reciprocal relationships that are satisfying and meaningful in your life.

I told clients often about what I call constructive manipulation. Unlike destructive manipulation that is used to coerce others and keep them in a victim role, constructive manipulation is what you can use on yourself to believe that you can get what you want and need in a relationship without feeling rejection or abandonment. It is carried out by directly confronting issues that create the feelings of rejection and abandonment, which, in turn, raises awareness of the behaviors of both parties in the relationship so you feel more in control. This skill can prevent a lifetime of emotional bankruptcy as it provides an objective evaluation of the roles being played so that they can be changed.

Your emotional toolbox will also include the ability to invest in yourself (and not in Prince Charming, whether or not he is in your life). Investing in yourself provides the emotional stability and intellectual capital for lifetime solvency. Don't hesitate to take the better job, to enroll in a class, to take that trip abroad, to volunteer in your community or church. All these behaviors contribute to your personal growth, self-confidence, and self-esteem while providing opportunities for building satisfying relationships across the spectrum of friends, family, and significant others. Relationships that are satisfying feed our emotional growth, build our emotional bank accounts' equity, and ensure sufficient emotional funds throughout life as a balanced emotional budget that pays serious interest and dividends.

Resiliency is a component in your new toolbox to build emotional solvency and build a strong emotional account. Resiliency is the ability to cope by using mental processes and behaviors that promote building personal assets and protect the self from potential negative effects. Resiliency, in most people, builds from childhood to adulthood as one learns how to respond to negative things that happen in our lives. It is apparent that resiliency is an individual trait that is different in each of us. But we can learn how to be more resilient by using certain behaviors that favor resilience as a trait. Connectivity, the ability to relate to others, is first. What is it that Barbra Streisand's song says, "People who need people, / Are the luckiest people in the world!" Yes, it is true, being connected to others is an asset. The emotionally bankrupt person is connected, but not in the way in which adds to one's being. Their connections are draining, not fulfilling.

In addition to connecting, resilience is built by being goal-oriented—setting small goals that integrate and bring about major accomplishments and bring you ultimately to where you want to be. Unlike the emotionally bankrupt person who is constantly revising goals to fit the relationship and has no time to attend to personal goals, the strong person who is emotionally solvent has a personal lifeline mapped out with clear directions in mind for how to achieve essential goals. Another asset held by the resilient person is decisiveness and positivity. The resilient person is *never* a victim. Despite how difficult or challenging life might become, resilience allows the person to bounce back many times with improved power and strength to overcome. Resilience brings perspective to any situation. Oftentimes, my clients could not see further than the relationship itself. Looking beyond what was happening was impossible; life was too overwhelming to get the other side where things could be better. In a way, all hope was often lost, and the ability to be optimistic or to visualize *how* things could be better was too difficult. As therapy progressed and the client got to this point with much encouragement and support, this self-discovery was often a turning point for real change. Never discount the value of self-care and hope as a part of restoring resilience.

CHAPTER 7

The Solvent You

Congratulations. You have taken the first steps to the solvent you by reading this book carefully and considering its application to your life. It if applies to you, hopefully you have made the decision to get out of emotional bankruptcy, build your new equity, invest in yourself, make regular deposits into your emotional account, and give up the victim role that has prevented your ability to being involved in healthy, productive relationships. The hope is that this book has brought empowerment and its advantages into your life. The sense of control that assures you that change is possible; that exiting your role as an emotionally bankrupt person is; and that you can achieve an emotionally solvent state with an account full of renewable assets achieved within meaningful relationships that bring love, caring, and reciprocity into your life on a daily basis. Empowerment does not mean you will be a control freak, telling others what to do and how to do it. It does not mean that you will become a selfish, self-centered individual who doesn't care about others. What it does mean is that you finally can be objective about others and how you relate to others in your everyday relationships. It means that you are self-confident, self-aware and that you will never allow anyone to make you feel like a victim again and that victim role is *not* where you want to be. Empowerment also means that you are committed to restoring your emotional solvency and are willing to build an emotional 401(k) that will protect your future in the same way your financial 401(k) does.

Keep adding to it, make it strong, protect it, and enjoy the dividends that it pays in your life.

At this point, you should have completed and reviewed the assessment in Chapter 4 and hopefully have begun to keep a journal to track your assets, liabilities, deposits and withdrawals in your everyday interactions. Soon it will all become so natural, it will not be necessary for you to do so; it will be comfortable and a part of your new role and behaviors. Soon you will see your choices in how you relate to others being those that are replenishing and rejuvenating. You will begin to reap the rewards of strong, functional relationships that meet your needs and build your self-esteem. You will feel empowered each day as your emotional solvency grows and develops. You will no longer be a victim by choice, but instead will be positive in your convictions about who you are as a person and celebrate your value as a person. You will be able to express your needs without guilt and will not feel selfish about considering the importance of your own needs. Remember, you are being the best possible person that you can be and that using those daily affirmations in the mirror each morning can set the stage for a productive and rewarding day each and every day.

Emotional bankruptcy is not a mental illness; it is a way of interacting with others that depletes energy and creates feelings of hopelessness, helplessness, and lack of self-confidence. The suggestions for reversing the process are contained in this book, and you can refer to them time and time again if you find yourself slipping back into the old ways of "overspending" in your emotional budget. The bankruptcy did not occur overnight, and the return to solvency will not happen that quickly either. Make the commitment to never mortgage your emotional account beyond its capacity ever again. I have faith in your commitment to want to be an individual who believes in her own self and in her self-worth and abilities to be both a giver and a receiver and to know the value of both sides of that process. Eliminate the idea that seeing both sides means you are selfish and uncaring. That is an old wives' tale long abandoned in the history of female growth and development.

You are a good and worthy person, a person who deserves to be treated with respect, honor, and care. Celebrate the new you. Don't be willing to accept any less!

GLOSSARY

Asset—a useful, valuable thing

Bankruptcy—A legal state of insolvency, the initiation of liquidation of assets in the process of bankruptcy (*chapter 7*), the initiation of reorganization proceedings in the process of bankruptcy (*chapter 11*), the rescheduling of debt and paying of debt over time in the process of bankruptcy (*chapter 13*).

Boundary—limit, a dividing line

Cognitive restructuring—The management of negative thinking with the replacement of positive, rational thinking.

Communication—the exchange of information and/or feelings

Debit—removal of money from an account

Dividend—a benefit of an action or a share of profits

Dischargeable debt—The process of allowing personal liability to be eliminated in the process of bankruptcy.

Emotional bankruptcy—Depletion of emotional energy as a result of maintaining nonreciprocal interpersonal relationships.

Equity—The value remaining after other payments and interests due are considered.

Insolvency—Liabilities exceed assets.

Liquidation—The selling off of assets.

Locus of Control—source of understanding of how events occur; external being outside of self, internal being within oneself

Overdraft—drawing more out of an account that the account holds

Reciprocity—the process of exchange for mutual benefit

Resilience—the capacity to recover quickly from a difficulty; ability to spring back from hardship

Self-esteem—confidence in personal worth and abilities

Solvency—having more assets than liabilities; the ability to pay debts

Voluntary bankruptcy—Bankruptcy filed by the one in debt.

EXERCISES FOR

RESTORING AND

MAINTAINING SOLVENCY

Exercise 1: Auditing assets (strengths) and liabilities (areas for growth)

This exercise is designed to help you to determine the strengths you can capitalize upon and the areas that need personal growth. It is helpful to do your audit at least every two months so that you can track the changes in your thinking and behavior that are moving you toward solvency and out of emotional bankruptcy.

Key is to be honest with yourself. Don't be afraid to acknowledge your strengths, be proud of them and use them to your benefit. Likewise, acknowledge the liabilities and work toward improving the ways in which you can diminish them in your interactions with others. You can use this exercise to provide motivation, encouragement and persistence in your efforts to toward a healthy emotional environment.

Exercise 1

Today's Date_____

ASSETS (list at least 3)   Liabilities (list at least 3)

Why did you choose the above as assets?

Why did you choose the above as liabilities?

How do you plan to continue to use the assets to your advantage?

How do you plan to improve the liabilities?

Exercise 2: Balancing the Books

The purpose of this exercise is to provide a mechanism for determining your process of give and take in your interpersonal relationships. If you remember in your reading, emotional bankruptcy occurs because there is much more "give" than "take" by the emotionally bankrupt person. It is the reasons your emotional account becomes depleted leaving you feeling exhausted, frustrated, angry, and helpless! This is what you are so earnestly attempting to change; therefore, it is so important that you keep track of maintaining a balance as you go through life. This exercise will help you to practice this behavior and be more mindful in your thinking to maintain the balance you need for healthy relationships.

Think of using the exercise in the same way you balance your checkbook…remember we want to avoid the overdrafts at all times!

Exercise 2   Balancing the Books

Under credits, identify thoughts and behaviors that build self-esteem
Under debits, identify thoughts and behaviors that diminish self-esteem.
Goal: at end of day, credits outweigh debits to equal a + score

Credits (+1 point each)	Debits (-1 point each)
Said yes because I wanted to	Said yes when I really meant no
Complimented myself at least once	Thought negatively about myself
Took time for me	Spent all day pleasing others
Refused to be a victim	Victim behaviors prevailed
Felt empowered from within	Allowed others to intimidate me
Began the day with affirmations	Unable to state affirmations
Followed my plan to erase emotional debt	Plan did not work today
Exercised and followed good nutrition	Too tired to exercise, ate junk
Felt positive about personal interactions	Difficulties interacting today
Confidence is growing	Confidence not improving

Had 7-8 hours of restful sleep	Sleep troubled and intermittent
Maintained boundaries	Boundaries violated
Made no excuses for others	Excusing unacceptable behavior
Felt in healthy control	Over controlling of others
Meditated or used yoga for relaxation	Too tense to acquire relaxation

(you may feel free to add other credits and debits from your day)

Total Credits_____   Total Debits_____

Balance score_____

Exercise 3: Mirror, mirror…Affirmations for growth

The goal of this exercise is to provide the cognitive practice opportunities for building self-esteem through the recitation of positive thought about oneself. Repeated statements when you are looking directly at yourself and concentrating on what it is you are saying can begin the cognitive change process for building self-confidence and positive thoughts about who you are as a person.

The exercise provides you with a sampling of statements, but as you become more comfortable with the exercise, you can add your own statements based on your personal needs. These should be done daily and ideally done in front of a mirror while directly looking at yourself.

Exercise 3   Mirror, mirror…Affirmations

I am a good person
I am worthy of respect from myself and others
I am worthy of love
I will not be a victim of others' anger or manipulation
I expect others to treat me fairly
I can be successful in my relationships
I will treat myself well today
I will not allow others to abuse me today in words or actions
I believe in myself and my abilities
I am making progress in improving my life
I am worthy of happiness
I am working toward being emotionally fit
I will communicate my needs to others without fear of retaliation
I cannot be everything to everyone
I trust my judgment
I am working to feel confident
I am becoming strong
I will reach my goal (state what it is)
I am a caring person
I will allow others to care for me when necessary
I have the power to change who I am
(add others based on your personal needs)

Exercise 4: Communication cues for clarity

Communication is a key element as you build personal emotional solvency. Communication is the interactive tool that lets others know what we need as well as providing a mechanism for information exchange that builds relationships. This exercise will offer options you can practice as you build the skills that empower your thinking and decision- making abilities. Open communication provides the opportunity to clearly consider choices and accept responsibility for how we relate to others. Without meaningful communication, relationships can be chaotic and facilitate emotional bankruptcy characterized by unmet needs, frustration, and victimization.

Practice these cues and become comfortable with using them with others at home, at work and in personal relationships. It is helpful to role play them first with a trusted friend or family member.

Write about using the cues in your journal. Share the successes and the difficulties.

Exercise 4   Communication cues for clarity

Verbal

Never begin a sentence with an apology
Use "I" statements as much as possible, especially in an argument or confrontation
Pause before you respond to a difficult question or request
Do not be afraid to say no if you do not want to say yes!
Listen carefully to what others are saying
Focus on the person speaking to you, use eye contact
Say what you mean clearly; say what you need clearly
Speak in a clear voice loud enough for others to hear you
Breathe
Ask for clarification if you are not sure what you heard the other person say
Be positive in your approach to others
Say thank you when receiving a compliment

Non-verbal

Stand tall (even if you are only 5' tall)
Maintain eye contact
Use color in your attire to augment your confidence
Be aware of facial gestures that are not in congruence with verbal comments
Use a firm handshake
Do not look down at the floor while speaking
Use self-talk to boost positivity
Decide what to do with your hands if you feel nervous
Smile

Exercise 5: Building a solid 401K

This exercise is at the heart of overcoming emotional bankruptcy because it allows for personal growth and a solid foundation for life-long solvency. Just like your financial 401K or other retirement plan, your emotional 401K protects your emotional future within relationships. This 401K invests in YOU. It is you that will experience the opportunity for change, lifelong resilience, and an environment of nurturing and caring.

Like any investment plan, it will grow over time. It takes patience to see the return on your investment and at times you need to be prepared for losses that may occur. However, you will be better prepared to deal with the losses if you have not exhausted your everyday supply of energy through behaviors that are characteristic of victimization rather than empowerment.

Practice, practice, practice. You can never overload the 401K.

Exercise 5   Building a solid 401K

1. Keep a solid balance by valuing yourself. You are a special person and you deserve to be good to yourself. Do at least one thing each day that makes you feel happy and proud of yourself.
2. Remember you consist of mind, body and spirit. Challenge your mind, take care of your body, and feed your spirit. Choose one of the follow suggestions each day/week/month to accomplish this:
   a. Take a walk, do yoga, join a gym
   b. Plan a week of nutritious meals, get that long overdue physical, try a new food
   c. Go on a personal retreat, meditate, take a spa day
3. Give of yourself honestly. Volunteer for a cause you support and believe in. Helping others does feed our soul when we initiate the kindness and do not feel manipulated by those you give to.
4. Call a friend you haven't spoken to in a while just to chat; send a handwritten note to someone special
5. If it fits into your lifestyle and you've been considering it, get a pet,
6. Remove toxic people, events, conversations from your life for good. Surround yourself with positive, good people. Cleansing your emotional environment will provide a sense of accomplishment and reduce overall stress

Be sure to journal the results of this exercise so that you can monitor your progress. Describe in the journal how carrying out these suggestions makes you feel. Enjoy the positive feelings. If negative results occur, examine what happened objectively and don't be afraid to try again.

Exercise 6: Let's sabotage stress

There are 100s of books, articles, blogs, and webinars that will attempt to teach you how to reduce personal stress. Most of these will tell you that stress affects every part of your mind, body and spirit and can cause heart disease, insomnia, gastrointestinal disorders, headaches, anxiety, and a multitude of other problems. Stress is a familiar event in the life of an emotionally bankrupt individual, and it interferes with everyday relationships at home, at work and in personal life. These exercises are used by many every day to decrease and manage stress. It is helpful to find a quiet spot in your home (or at your workplace if also a stressful environment) to carry out the exercises.

Controlling stress then is an important means of getting out of emotional debt, maintaining a balanced emotional budget, and returning to solvency. Below are some stress relieving strategies that are simple, yet an effective quick method to getting stress under control. Again, practice and persistence in utilizing them are what makes them work. Stress has built over time so time is needed to reverse that process. I encourage you to try them and enjoy the journey.

Exercise 6   Let's Sabotage Stress

Breathing

Deep breathing is extremely helpful when stressed or feeling tense.

Take a breath that is deep enough to expand your abdomen and hold for at least 3 seconds.

Exhale all at once and while doing so relax your shoulders. Try to keep you mind clear of stressful thoughts and combine this breathing with imagery of a calm ocean breeze or soft waves lapping on the shore.

Repeat several times until you feel less tense.

Mindfulness

Assume a comfortable position, preferably sitting with good back support and feet on the floor. Each time you do this exercise, select the same spot if you can. Make it your spot to decompress

Close your eyes and concentrate on the present; get in touch with each part of your body and see it relaxing and letting go of the tension you are feeling. Keep going until you have eased the tension in each part of your body: jaw, neck, shoulders, arms, chest, abdomen, legs, ankles, feet, toes. As you are doing so become aware of the sensations around you.

Open your eyes slowly, reconnect to your surroundings, take a few cleansing deep breaths.

You may choose to play quiet music if you like. Classical music works very well for this exercise.

Mind/Spirit/Creativity

Choose an activity you enjoy that allows for creative expression of your true self.

Some suggestions are painting, reading, listening to music, hiking outdoors, writing or daydreaming.

Each week select an activity that can help you "escape for about 30 minutes of time without interruption. One of my clients created artistic collages to express conflicted feelings. She would bring them to our sessions for discussion which helped her to gain insight to internal stressors.

Working with clay, needlepoint, knitting can also reduce stress especially when accompanied by soft music

Take a bubble bath and daydream without limits!

Exercise 7: Testing your resilience

This exercise is designed to be used about every 3 months to determine your progress in building emotional resilience. When emotional bankruptcy occurs, resilience is at an all-time low due to depleted energy, high anxiety, low self-esteem and inability to express feelings for fear of abandonment. The goal then is to build our capacity for resilience through reflection on what is happening around us and influences our life. This exercise requires a commitment to be honest in your reflections and to learn new ways of responding. Remember in your reading, you are exiting the role of victim and accepting the role of empowerment. That is a dramatic change that will not happen overnight, but practicing the processes in the book and in these exercises will build that capacity for resilience over time until it becomes a natural part of you.

Review the following questions at least every 3 months or more often if you feel the need to do so. Record your responses on the exercise sheet or in your journal. Remember the integrity of your answers makes progress easier.

Exercise 7   Testing your resilience

Today's Date_____

1. What positive thoughts did you have today? How did those thoughts make you feel?

2. What negative thoughts did you have today? What did those thoughts relate to? How did those thoughts make you feel? What steps did you take to reverse the negative thinking? Did they work? Why or why not? What would you do differently next time if they did not work?

3. Were your personal needs met today through your relationships? Were you able to ask for help if you needed it? Was asking for help easier for you today than in the past? What has changed that has allowed you to ask for help?

4. What was the most stressful event for you today? How did you respond to that stress? Were you satisfied with your response? If not, what will you do differently next time?

5. Do you feel emotionally stronger today? What makes you feel stronger? What are you still working on to improve your resilience?

6. On a scale of 1-10, with 1 being least resilient, and 10 being most resilient, how would you score yourself today?

Exercise 8: Avoiding Victim Mentality

Being emotionally bankrupt and having victim mentality are synonymous. In chapter we examined the characteristic of being a victim vs. feeling empowered. This exercise will assist you in determining when you choose to be the victim rather than being empowered within your relationships.

Each time you make the choice to be the victim, you are withdrawing from your emotional account; you are creating a debit rather than a credit. You are feeding the passive, pushover, pawn person inside of you rather than empowering the courageous, confident, and strong convicted being within.

As you make the effort to do this exercise it can be painful and it can resurrect sad, discouraging feelings you would rather ignore than face. Remember, no one can make you a victim, you choose that role. Use this exercise to EXIT the role and to embrace the new role of empowerment.

Exercise 8   Avoiding victim mentality

Today's date_____

Situation for analysis

Think about an event that occurred in the past week where you choose to be the victim. Can you picture what happened? Can you write down in your journal the steps that led to you choosing to be the victim? What were the triggers you can identify that moved you into the victim role?

How did you feel being the victim in this situation? Did you take any steps toward feeling empowered rather than victimized? Where in the following cycle did you make that attempt?

Self-pity (victim)>>>giving up>>>>staying stuck>>>>pushing others away>>>>decreased self-esteem (staying the victim)

What could you have done to turn around the event and be empowered?

Exercise 9: Staying in your Lane...
Oh those boundaries

The idea of locus of control discussed in the introduction of the book provides some insight into how one looks at where the concept of control lives in our world. Some believe that what happens to us is controlled by our inner self (internal locus), while others feel it is the environment or others that control what happens (external locus). The person experiencing emotional bankruptcy, who often plays the victim as seen in the previous exercise, has difficulty understanding the boundaries of life. Where do I end and you begin is often a mystery. As a result, boundaries of interacting and relationships are often violated which can lead to feelings of anger, anxiety, and frustration.

In this exercise, the reader will have an opportunity to test the boundaries of a simple relationship situation. It is also helpful to think about how you respond to the thought of "staying in your lane" when interacting with others whether at home, at work, or in personal relationships. Overstepping boundaries and feeling the need to control others is also a debit in your emotional budget. It can be draining to feel that you must control everything and everyone. Oftentimes despite playing the "poor me victim", that role in itself is a method of controlling others.

Let's build the deposits in the emotional account by knowing when to sit back and let a situation play out to its natural end. Spending our assets on the need for control will not ensure emotional integrity and contradict the need to invest in yourself daily.

Exercise 9 Staying in your lane…
Oh those boundaries

Jim and Louise have been in a relationship for the past two years. They live together and work at the same company. Jim is a junior executive and Louise is a marketing guru. Jim is vying for a major promotion and has been working overtime to build his case as the best man for the job. Louise is not happy that she is being ignored and has been whiney and often complains that she is "second in line" to his job. On the other hand she tells him she wants him to get the promotion so that they can move to a bigger apartment. Louise, without Jim's knowledge, talks to a colleague she is friendly with in the department where Jim has applied for the promotion to "put in a good word and vouch for his abilities". Jim inadvertently finds out and is furious that Louise interfered in his work. She accuses him of not appreciating her wanting to help him get the promotion and to ultimately have a good outcome for both of them. She tells him he is selfish and he argues that she has to have her hand in everything. The argument becomes serious and now Louise is full of self-pity and is questioning if Jim really loves her after all. She says his stubbornness is ruining the relationship, and he responds that her intrusiveness is compromising his career.

What are the issues in this scenario? Can you identify with Louise's feelings about the outcome of her "assistance"? Should Jim be more understanding here?

Does this scenario sound familiar to you? Is there a similar scenario in your past relationships? Do you remember how you felt at that time?

If a similar scenario arose today in a work, home or personal relationship, how would you handle it? What would make the difference now?

How would you define your present locus of control? Is there a need to change it? Why or why not? What does control signify to you?

Exercise 10: The Solvent You

Exercise 10 is a maintenance exercise. It is designed to be used on an ongoing basis to examine whether you are sustaining the solvency of your emotional bank account. It appraises your growing assets and healthy emotional deposits. It ascertains that you are maintaining a balanced emotional budget without overdrafts and foolish emotional spending. It encourages that you are investing in yourself daily and saving for a rainy day by paying yourself first. It ensures that you are staying out of emotional debt and avoiding future bankruptcy.

This exercise is meant to be used anytime you believe you need a check-up! Yes, regular check-ups in this realm are just as important as your yearly mammogram, physical, and regular maintenance on your automobile. New behaviors and cognitive thought patterns can sometimes slip back into previous behavior especially when you are particularly stressed.

Don't be afraid to use this or any of the ten exercises whenever you feel the need. It does not mean you are not being successful in avoiding bankruptcy. On the contrary, I see it as your means of preventing a future emotional bankruptcy from happening. I see the responses to this exercise important to add to your journal so that you have a means of comparison over time when monitoring your progress toward the solvent you.

So, build that credit, feed that 401K, keep investing in yourself. You are worth it.

Exercise 10 The Solvent You

Today's date_____

How would you compare your emotional bank account today vs. six months ago?

What would you consider the most important change you have made within your relationships?

What are you continuing to work on to improve your emotional bank account?

How have you changed as a person in the last 6 months?

What are your long-term goals for family relationships? For work relationships? For personal relationships?

How did you utilize the exit-role theory to leave the victim role and move to the empowered role? What was the motivation? What were the barriers?

REFERENCES

Adutltmeducation. 2018. "Facilitating Behavior Change." Retrieved at adultmeducation.com/facilitatingbehaviorchange.html.

Adultmeducation. 2018. "Readiness to Change." Retrieved at adult-meducation.com/downloads/Readiness-to-change_TOOL.pdf.

DiClemente and Prochaska. 1998. "Toward a Comprehensive trans-theoretical model of change." In *Treating Addictive Behavior*, Miller and Heather. 2nd ed. New York: Plenum.

Ebaugh, Helen Rose. 1988. *Becoming an Ex: The Process of Role Exit Theory*. Chicago: University of Chicago Press.

Fitzgerald, F. Scott. 1936. *The Crack-Up. Esquire*. Retrieved at http://www.sc.edu/fitzgerald/facts/facts5.html.

Gambardella, Lucille C. 2008. "Role Exit Theory and Marital Discord Following Extended Military Deployment." *Perspectives in Psychiatric Care*, vol. 44, issue 3, pp. 169–174.

Tabor, PA and DA Lopez. 2004. "Improving Medical Adherence." *Journal of Pharmacology Practice*, vol. 3, pp. 167–81.

Zimmerman, et al. 2000. "Intervention to Improve Medical Adherence." *American Journal of Psychiatry*, 159, pp. 1653–54.

ABOUT THE AUTHOR

Dr. Lucille Gambardella is an accomplished leader in nursing education and a licensed and certified advanced practice nurse specialist in psychiatric/mental health practice. Over the past forty years, Lucille has been instrumental in helping depressed women recognize the phenomenon of "emotional bankruptcy" in their lives and by facilitating solutions for restoring "emotional solvency" and the ability to establish quality relationships with others.

Dr. Gambardella is a graduate of Villanova University, Boston University, and Columbia Pacific University and is a certified nurse educator by the National League for Nursing, as well as a certified advanced practice nurse by the American Nurses Credentialing Center. In addition, Lucille is recognized as a Fellow by the Academy of Nursing Education and was named the first Nurse Legend in the state of Delaware by the Delaware Nurses Association and the Delaware Organization of Nurse Executives and Leaders. Dr. Gambardella has presented her work internationally, nationally, and locally at health-care venues for public and professional audiences. She is married to her husband, Bob, for forty-nine years and has two daughters, Gina and Andrea. She enjoys living at the beach in Lewes, Delaware.

CPSIA information can be obtained
at www.ICGtesting.com
Printed in the USA
JSHW010625050220
4022JS00001B/7